Sport
The Opiate
of The People?

by
Peter Ballantine
Priest in Charge Clifton upon Dunsmore and Newton and Churchover with Willey, Coventry Diocese

GROVE BOOKS LIMITED
Bramcote   Nottingham   NG9 3DS

CONTENTS

1. Questions of Sport 3
2. '... Like Kissing Your Sister' 4
3. 'Critics of Football are ... Commies' 6
4. 'More Serious Than Life or Death' 12
5. 'Like War without Killing' 14
6. 'Opiate for the Masses' 16
7. Run the Straight Race—In Conclusion 24

Copyright Peter Ballantine 1988

PREFACE

My thanks to Dr. Wilf Murphy who first asked me to give some lectures to his students on the Sports Science degree at Liverpool Polytechnic, to the Grove Ethics Group who helped me rush this work out and to Mary Yorke who valiantly typed the manuscript under trying circumstances.

THE COVER PICTURE

is by Greg Forster

First Impression July 1988
ISSN 0262-799X
ISBN 1 85174 087 2

1. QUESTIONS OF SPORT

Sport is a major part of our modern life—it takes up many hours of T.V. and radio, back pages of newspapers are full of it, advertising feels there are benefits in sponsorship or using famous sporting personalities. Sport may even affect national and international consciousness.

It has become a truism in recent years to note the increased leisure time available to us, whether for those in paid employment or for the many without work. We all use (and are being encouraged to use) leisure facilities and many find their enjoyment through being spectators. Many people, Christians included, are employed in the sporting industry.

But sport is not value-free and has ideologies, some very obvious, some not so. Down the ages the Christian church has used sport to preach a message to society. A most obvious example is the 'muscular Christianity' movement of the nineteenth century. Secular society also has been and is using sport to say certain things to its own societies. The Christian church must work out its attitudes to sport as in many other aspects of life. God is creator and ruler of all and no area of life can be shielded from his gaze. We are encouraged through Christ to have a 'renewing of our minds' (Romans 12.2) and that must work for all our attitudes and the influences on us. The power of sport and its place in our conscious is now a matter for academic study. These thought starters (this booklet claims no great originality and recognizes that the real work has yet to be written) originated from a few lectures the author gave on 'Religion and Sport' to Sport Scientist students at Liverpool Polytechnic when he was Chaplain there. Others have given critical analyses from varying viewpoints (e.g. Garry Whannel writes from a left-wing viewpoint[1]).

The challenge is to the Christian church to do likewise.

A Definition

There is little difficulty in describing soccer, rugby, cricket, baseball as sport—but what about chess, clay pigeon shooting, foxhunting? Where does one draw the line? Is it the element of physical competition? But does not sport involve the mental as well—and does competition mean that the modern idea of non-competitive games are not really sport at all? My tentative definition of sport is 'a particular way of using leisure time in a combination of physical and mental skills in a competitive way leading to a set of aims/goals by which the contest is won or lost.' By this very definition the idea of competition is introduced and taken as axiomatic in sport. There may be sporting skills used in similar activities such as cooperative games but I would suggest that these are fun (and fun would also be in sport obviously) and well worthwhile for that, and not inferior but a different activity. This is not to suggest that I am not unaware of the drawbacks of competition or to say that sport has taken on some undesirable attributes. This is not to deny 'fun games' and their value—it is not an either/or but a both/and serving differing roles.

---

[1] *Blowing the Whistle* (Pluto Press, 1983).

2. '... LIKE KISSING YOUR SISTER'

The Values of Competition

What are the supposed advantages of competition in sport? Team co-operation has often been highlighted as a function of competition which is healthy. The idea of working together (of course this does not apply to more individual sports) for a common goal brings out a corporate spirit in people. As Christians, the idea of team work should appeal immensely. Having opponents gives you the yardstick against which to measure yourself and your goals. Having opponents is a spur to improve and achieve. Having this standard encourages the team to endeavour to see each member reaches his or her potential.

In its ideal, losing in such circumstances does not need to be demeaning. The pleasure of trying, of doing, of having fun can be sufficient. As a member of the school house team that always came bottom each year in the football competition (and most others) my pleasure was not diminished by the lack of results. It was the pleasure of having a 'go'. This indeed may be particularly true of amateur sport and certainly raises questions of professional sport where, by its very nature, the necessity of success is built in. Enjoyment of physical and mental effort is surely some reflection of our joy in being created beings and with these endowments and making use of them. Questions may be asked of people being equal. Not all people are gifted sportingly or have an interest in it. One feels for many a sensitive person (or simply people whose eyesight is not that good to see a ball) who have been forced to play sport and not enjoyed one moment of it. That is clearly not right—but those who gain pleasure in sport, or have talents that way, surely should be allowed to enjoy themselves that way? Or, if they are like me, they may get vicarious enjoyment through being a spectator!

Competition at its best does produce excellence (who can but admire Daley Thompson?), beauty (from acrobatics and figure-skating to watching a Maradonna glide through a defence), courage (a Bert Trautman who plays through a cup final with a broken neck) and dedication (an athlete who spends many hours in training). All these surely show something of God's creativity in man?

God created us with minds and bodies. Enjoyment of physical and mental effort is surely a reflection of our joy in his creation. This may be true in amateur sport. Whether it can be true of professional sport, which has a built-in demand for success, is open to question.

Competition gives pleasure and a sense of pride (in the best sense of that word) to the spectator. Paul was proud after all of being a citizen of no mean city. Sometimes it is virtually the only thing your locality can have some pride in—not least Liverpool. One wonders what would happen to the morale of that city if both teams declined.

Other defences of competition in sport are more dubious. There is the idea that sport 'contains' violence. American football is said to be 'violence within the rules' and thus presumably through a vicarious enjoyment of that kind of violence reduces its actuality outside the game. One could turn that argument on its head and say that football (American style) is merely a reflection of a violent society (which the USA certainly is). There is no hard evidence to prove or disprove such an assertion—it is simply a wild generalization. Some may even say that the evidence in this instance is that American football is linked to the ultimate kind of violence—militarism.

The 'win at all costs' syndrome can result in violence on the pitch. The remark of the famous American football coach that a moral victory (but losing the game) is 'like kissing your sister', is a witty way of putting it. 'How can you be proud of a losing team?' said Jim Tatum, a college football coach in the USA. Does this say something about sport in itself or the societies that spawn it? Paul Gardner[1] says 'I believe that football ... tends to instill into men the feeling that victory comes through hard, almost slavish work, teamplay, self-confidence and an enthusiasm that amounts to dedication.' Truly this is a picture of the American ethic of work?

---

[1] *Nice Guys Finish Last* (Allen Lane, 1974).

3. 'CRITICS OF FOOTBALL ARE ... COMMIES'

Sport and ideology
The link between sport and religion and politics in the ancient world has been well documented. The Egyptian goddess Sehet was worshipped as the goddess of Sport and the crowning glory of the Greek sport ideal was the Olympic games which presupposed a 'holy peace'. Or in Rome there arose a close link between the gladiatorial type games and the triumphant concept of empire. Victory in the arena was an expression of Roman power in the field. And of course Christians, themselves, were victims in these arenas and their destruction a symbol of Rome's destruction of any group that might threaten its existence. Such sport carried very clear messages.

Sport in England
A look at aspects of our national history can be instructive.

(a) The *Pre-Reformation* period is seen as a time when the church was the centre of society around which much of the leisure slot focussed. After all, 'holiday' is a corruption of 'Holy Day' of which there were a great many. Festivities would include much of what later became our more formal sport such as the very rough football brawls. However much of the competition would be linked to the military—archery, fencing and the like—and reminds us of the strong link there has been between sport and the military down the ages. This was reflected in the ambivalence to such tournaments by the Papacy e.g. Second Lateran Council of 1139 passed an interdict against them but by 1316 John XXII allowed them! Nevertheless many monastic orders did encourage sport.

(b) The changes of the *Reformation* period affected the fabric of society itself. The abolition of the monastic system, the reduction in holy days and in ceremonial began the secularization of society. The alleged shortcomings of the monastic clergy at the time of the dissolution of the monasteries and the felt shortcomings of the post-reformation clergy (as strongly perceived by the Puritans) led to a reaction against 'merrie England'. One puritan complained before Queen Elizabeth about some clergy 'some shake bucklers, some ruffians, some hawkers and hunters, some dicers and carders . . .' One of the clergy deprived in 1643 at the time of the Civil War was described as . . . 'football playing and other ungodly practices'. The puritans' objections to the Popish origins of much activity and the low standards of clergy simply meant that their activities were seen in a low light. One of the biggest clashes between the puritans and the monarchy was over Sabbath observance—the puritans were outraged at the *Book of Sports* (1617) which allowed games on Sunday after divine service. Perhaps the puritans' image of the 'gloomy England' has been overstated—William Perkins, a leading divine, was not opposed to games and recreation as long as they did not lead to excesses and were decorous. Sports certainly survived during the Commonwealth period and it is to the puritans' credit that they objected to blood sports such as bear-baiting, though one cynic later wrote, 'the puritans objected to bear-baiting not so much because of the pain it gave to the bears but to the pleasure it gave to the spectators.'

(c) Nevertheless the *Restoration* of 1660 and subsequent 150 years led to a partial restoration of games and sports. Henry Newcombe noticed at Oakham a morris dance in 1660, 'which I had not seen of 20 years before'. The period saw the church replaced as the centre of social life by the almshouse, and sports arose away from church influence. Local lords might sponsor sports, as e.g. cricket, in the eighteenth century, which also saw the rise of horse-racing and boxing. The Sabbath question remained a source of contention (Acts of 1780) which led to a decline of the more violent sports on that day.

(d) The period of the *Industrial Revolution,* at least in the early years of the nineteenth century, is often seen as a black period for leisure and sport when sports were discouraged in the bigger and growing cities, partly because of new long working hours for the industrial proletariat and partly because of ill health in the slums[1] and partly the sheer lack of open spaces. But what we do see as the century progresses is a rebirth of sport in the way that we largely know it today.[2]

Older chaotic sports such as soccer with its vague and variable rules gradually get codified and limited to set playing areas. Older versions such as Ashbourne survive as an anachronism. Formal competitions arise with games at regular periods, e.g. on Saturday afternoons, and mass spectator sports (although gates of 20,000 for cricket in the eighteenth century were not unknown) take off.

This raises the question of 'social engineering'. How much was sport regularized, tamed, codified to fit into a new industrial regime? Sport is now a feature of the town with its new disciplines and limited space as opposed to the more disorganized chaotic country ideal. This social engineering was underlined by the church which now returns to the centre of the stage (partly as a result of the revivals of the eighteenth and nineteenth centuries). Into this situation comes 'Muscular Christianity', largely a product of the public school system. Part of this Christian revival is linked to a cult of games and sport.

It is worthwhile spending some time on this subject since the ethos of muscular Christianity is still with us today if only in attenuated form. Games and sport were introduced to some public schools in the middle of the nineteenth century as a form of social control in what had been anarchic situations. Cyril Norwood said 'Cotton went to Marlborough to create a school out of mutineers and he consciously developed organized games as one of the methods by which the school should be brought to order.'

As the games movement developed so its ideology developed—an emphasis that games lead to manliness (a reaction agianst what was seen as effeminate Puseyism?)—courage, despising of pain. A good sport played within the rules and did not complain. Success on the sports field was seen as a preparation for life with its discipline and teamwork. *Mens sana in corpore sano* was the motto of the movement. Many trained at these schools were ordained, and tried in the parishes and mission field to

---
[1] e.g. Engels *Conditions of the Working Class in England* (1844).
[2] e.g. M. Cunningham *Leisure in the Industrial Revolution* (Croom Helm, London, 1980).

work out these principles. Such an example is Cecil Earle Tyndale Briscoe who worked at a CMS school in Kashmir from 1890 to 1947. Someone described him as the 'imperial standard bearer of Victorian moral righteousness'. Clearly he was a man of courage—during a cholera epidemic he with students would fill up cesspools and clean streets—and had a fair amount of compassion; but it was linked with insensitivity (e.g. making Hindus play with a leather ball—one boy was not allowed back home because by kicking it he was defiled) and extreme arrogance. The dilemmas of imperialism passed him by.[1] For him athletics created muscle and skill to fight evil and promote good.

This might be an extreme example but the message was brought into all parts of the nation and empire. Several football clubs had their origins in church groups (e.g. Aston Villa and Everton).

Through sport people's lives were being trained, the body tamed (more than a hint of sexual suppression?) bodies and minds trained for the empire, for playing one's part in society, as those with power saw it.

One can make many comments about such a movement, not least to ask how Christian it was with its ideal of the 'gentleman', with its training for the empire, snobbery and sheer naivety. One public school magazine writes:

'How many a charge through the ranks of the foe
have been made by the warrior who years ago
hurried the leather from hand to hand . . .'

The Somme is a tragic finale to this way of thinking. However, it lingers on with our idea of the good sport, sportsmanship and love of physical strength (how brutal were those Victorian games!—see *Tom Brown's Schooldays*).

One can comment that the Lord has no delight in a man's legs (Psalm 147.16)—there was almost an idolatry of physical strength and manliness. There was a lack of a social justice—the system was unquestioned. Or what of the child who did not like games, who was not 'tough'—does that devalue him?

By the *twentieth century* we see sports flourishing in their modern form and certainly very secularized. In this country, for the most part the church has withdrawn from competing, though Christian colleges in the USA have a very high place for sports and sporting success. We now have the emphasis on winning, at times at all costs. No longer is merely taking part enough, certainly where sport is in very commercial or professional hands. The question is: are Christians subconsciously taking in secular values via sport?

Who is Using Sport Today?

In the year of the Olympics we might be tempted to think of the positive values of sport as a bringing together of the nations in friendly competition. There is evidence that the Olympic Games revival from 1896 has

---

[1] See *Christ and the Imperial Games Field;* 'Evangelical Athletes of the Empire by J. A. Morgan in British Journal of Sports Science Vol. 1, No. 2 (Sept. 1984).

achieved some of this ideal, but it is an ideal that had become sadly twisted in recent years. Prestige now accrues to the host nation which provides the lavish facilities. Lord Killanin, involved in the Olympic movement for many years, (president 1972-80) regretting the changes, notes that Melbourne (1956) was the last of the 'old style' Olympics. The Montreal complex (1976) cost billions and was barely ready on time. What is the morality of a nation like Mexico spending vast sums on prestige facilities when so many of the inhabitants are so poor?

One can obviously point to earlier abuses of the Olympic ideal—notably Hitler's use of the 1936 Games to prove Aryan supremacy. In recent times states like East Germany seem to use sport almost as a weapon of national identity. Here is a way that a contrived political unit gains international cohesion and pride through sporting success as it brings esteem on the world stage. Because teams are largely 'national', their success or failure becomes a source of national pride or shame.

Sport in fact becomes an agent of the 'cold war'. Boycotts become part of international politicking, whether of the USA's cutting the 1980 Moscow Olympics (as a protest against Afghanistan) or the USSR's withdrawal from the 1984 Los Angeles Olympics. Further to this is the blatant use by presidential candidates of the publicity attendant on being seen with the medal winners. It is no longer simply a question of taking part—it is also nationalism as well. The classic example of politics and sport is of course South Africa—increasingly isolated in the sporting field as in other aspects of life. Boycotts are of course always inconsistent. Why should Mrs. Thatcher encourage British athletes to boycott Moscow but want to encourage links with South Africa? And on this complex issue, if a team is truly to be a reflection of the nation as a whole, then it must in reality reflect it and not be an expression of just the section that has the hegemony.

On the Local Level

But politics also intervenes at the local level. The question of 'social engineering' again raises its head. Riots in areas like Toxteth (1981) produce trees and sports halls but no jobs. Garry Whannel (*op. cit.*) comments sarcastically, 'Nothing loosens the purse strings like panic'. A left-wing critique (and maybe it should be a Christian critique) would suggest that this is part of the state/establishment using sport to hide certain inequalities and deficiencies in society—what might be called a modern 'bread and circuses' syndrome. By this you get a docile labour force and unemployed cohort. Many from various walks of life have great hopes of leisure and sport in the light of what seems like long-term unemployment. With the present working revolution and need for less jobs (particularly at the 'lower' and 'less skilled' end of the working population), there will be need to offer more facilities for leisure and sport for people who are not currently needed in the labour force to have and enjoy fulfilled lives through such interests. Mrs. Mary Warnock in a symposium argues that leisure means the freedom to do what you like and thus you should do something.[1] You should like it and think it worth doing. She encourages us to develop a skill, e.g. golf, and an absorbing interest. This presumably means that we will find our increasing free time meaningful.

---

[1] *Leisure in the 1980s* (Proceedings University of Salford, 1980).

SPORT—THE OPIATE OF THE PEOPLE?
Is Sport the Answer?
However such ideas raise basic questions about the relationship of sport/ leisure to work. Traditionally we have thought of the leisure slot as the time when we are not doing our work. That is its definition and its meaning and *raison d'etre*. It relates to a balance between the two. Leisure was seen as 'fun', the time to get apart from the serious matters of life. Because it was fun it had no long-term goal. The famous historian Huizinga defined sport as the spontaneous and unpredictable release from the pressures of working life. If we remove the working life, how can 'fun', 'leisure' and 'sport' be a release? Are people going to find real long-term goals in leisure? Or as Aneurin Bevan once pointed out—are we in danger of introducing a new 'puritanism' into sport. It now has become 'serious' rather than 'fun'. Are we going to make 'leisure/sport' into simply another kind of 'work' with goals inherent of great seriousness? The 'protestant work ethic' may be re-emerging in another guise.

Furthermore, will the kind of person who has been the most vulnerable in this work recession, i.e. the casual labourer (using 'labour' in a wider connotation), want to be disciplined into this kind of sport? There are those who love to be in regular teams, compete in leagues and take their 'fun' 'seriously' in this respect, but many have a 'casual' attitude to 'fun' and would rather 'pick and choose' and have what would be in many eyes very short goals to their leisure. One could see this in the East End for instance—some youngsters preferred to go to clubs that had well organized teams while others would go to a place like the Mayflower Centre with its more 'kick about' attitude to games. Another reason why it may not all work like it is hoped is this: who are the people who are actually using the recently provided facilities? The unemployed may get cheap or free entrance and the facilities may be open all day, but the equipment still has to be bought, the socializing that attends such activities still has to be paid for. If you are surviving on state money, there is not much spare. Seeing car parks full outside some, e.g. Liverpool, sports centres and knowing that there are few cars in the neighbourhood, one asks questions about the status of users. Locals have expressed feelings (rightly or wrongly) that they simply are not really welcome.

There is in all this dangers of generalizing. There are those who enjoy their work and find it in itself almost a form of leisure. There are those who hate their work (workers on production lines?) who cannot wait for their leisure slot. People vary in their expectations and pleasures and capacities and this must be borne in mind. Sport cannot be a single panacea. Behind this kind of hope for sport may well be a fear re-emerging in a secular form of 'the devil finding things for those with idle hands to do'. Those in power want to curb the potential aggro and do 'good' to those they may fear by providing diversions from the wider issues of life. John Hargreaves says of modern sport:
> 'it is a middle class movement concerned with planning other people's cultural pursuits in order to ensure they get up to no radical mischief!'[1]

One writer has even said 'Sport is the opiate of the masses'. At one stage it was the church which allowed itself to be dragged into that situation. Maybe the church has learnt some of the lessons. We must be on our guard that sport does not go the same way.

[1] J. Hargreaves *Sport, Culture and Ideology* (R. & K. Paul, 1982).

So what about the women?
The issue of women's lib is as important in sport as anywhere else. It is not just a question of women's access to sport and sporting facilities (important though that is), but the very ethos of much of our modern sport. Basically, its macho image—that the successful sports person is virile, strong, even violent—is the very opposite of so-called 'feminine' attributes. Maybe the idea of the 'new man' who takes on some of these so-called feminine attributes may influence our idea of the sporting hero. Nothing is more pathetic than, say, the rugby player who has to show his virility by excessive displays of drunkenness with the resulting violence and stupidity and often sexism.

Rosemary Deem notes these reasons for women's difficulties in entering sport.[1] She notes the very 'macho' image itself as a barrier but also the traditional female role as the home maker. She may wash the kit, be the scorer (I can remember my mother keeping cricket score for my father's works team), or simply have to come along for the ride with the kids. There comes to mind the 'tug of war' where every summer Sunday in certain parts of the country is taken up with this male-dominated game.

On the other hand, males can be threatened by females and try to keep them from certain sports like the marathon. This may be reinforced by the feeling (held even by women) that they are physically inferior; but this is gradually being disproved as women's results get nearer men's. Some women may even be embarrassed about their own bodies after childbirth. Women may even at school be kept to 'feminine' sports e.g. the 'non-competitive' such as jogging, yoga, swimming, badminton. Somehow it is 'unfeminine' to get 'stuck in', get dirty or even sweat!

There again, women have to face up to sexism of the cruder sort in sport as any other facet of society. Kathy Switzer was sexually harassed when she was the first woman to run the 1967 Boston Marathon.

This differential can be seen in purely commercial terms. Why are women's prizes, e.g. at Wimbledon, less in value than men's?

Christians are having to rethink their gender roles (which in itself is many Grove Booklets), but they ought to have a holistic world-view and see what issues inter-relate in all facets of life. Not least, sport and feminism are a prime example of it.

And the blacks?
Many blacks would say that they have been stereotyped into sport at the expense of academic work, not least amongst afro-carribeans. Teachers, it is claimed, subconsciously have the idea that sport is the area of black prowess. Images of the black man as physically strong, and sexually virile have bitten deep into our thinking. It is further claimed that for the black person to succeed he/she has to be really good, whereas a mediocre white man would get through. One can point to how slowly blacks were accepted into American professional sport or to the racial chanting that many black sportsmen have to undergo in this country. Sport again is an expression of wider values.

[1] R. Deem *Sociology of Women and Leisure* (Open University Press, 1986).

4. 'MORE SERIOUS THAN LIFE OR DEATH'

Idolatry in Sport
'Football is not a matter of life and death—it's more serious than that'. Those are the often quoted words (tongue in cheek?) of Bill Shankley, the former manager of Liverpool football club. Sport has taken on a seriousness in this last part of the twentieth century that many question and Christians themselves should be asking.

The influence of the media and the greater rewards for success, both financial and prestigious, have given rise to the cult of the 'superstar' and the 'ego building'. Now personalities are front-page news for their sporting prowess and even their private lives are part of the 'circus'. Is this edifying for those directly involved—a George Best clearly could not cope. Is it a good example for those who follow the antics—what sense of values and worth does it give them and what does it say about society's values in general? Questions are raised about people in public life being examples to others—politicians, royalty, churchmen and the like. Do we ask the same of sportsmen/women?

Self-esteem
The Christian will want to ask questions about 'hubris'—man's pride in himself as opposed to in his God. It is a pride that is very fleeting, as peak physical fitness does not last that long, and anyway we all have to face death and judgment (Hebrews 9.27). To succeed at the very top must involve a great belief in yourself, and your ability can be an 'ego trip' indeed. Really to do well may involve a despising of others—this may simply be a ritual as in pre-big-boxing-fight ballyhoo but maybe the word of Jesus about calling your brother 'raca' has some relevance; and if it is purely 'hype' to make money and sell tickets then other questions of morality are relevant.

The very demands of training to achieve such peaks of fitness and fame become an obsession that is life-consuming and centred in on self-reward. A Christian may again want to ask questions about this type of involvement. Does it shirk all other issues of life that God wants us to be involved in? A response may be that such training is only for a small span of one's life, there is time for other matters later.

Yet for many this time of total commitment can last for years—over what St. Paul would call a crown that will not last (1 Corinthians 9.25).

The body
The demands of success may not only damage a man's true estimate of himself by overvaluing one aspect of his make-up and making him set a poor example for others, but they may, in the end, harm the body.

It is no longer a matter of keeping fit (in itself nothing for the Christian to undervalue) but exploiting and abusing the body for short-term goals. The scandal of drugs in sport is becoming increasingly open—not least the recent case of the British Olympic silver medallist David Jenkins being imprisoned in the USA for supplying cortizone drugs to the US sporting scene. Not that it is a problem of the West only—for years it has been claimed that Iron Curtain countries having been doing much the same. Drugs are available that delay puberty for girl gymnastic athletes so that they retain a slender figure. In many countries the aforementioned steroids are used to build up muscle power though with serious side-effects e.g. on the kidneys, reproductive organs, and other internal organs. Professional soccer players are encouraged to play when not totally fit with the long-term effects of arthritis. Not only do we ask whether this is true competition of body and mind but whether the long-term physical (mental?) effects really are worth it? What value success which is contrived and also destructive? Will victory in the next hundred years be achieved in the laboratory or on the field? A brave new world indeed!

The Media

All these difficulties are magnified by a media circus which increasingly looks for sordid titbits. No longer is it a description of the game, the players and their skill, but investigations into private lives—whether Ian Botham's drug-taking or David Pleat's nocturnal drives in seedy parts of London. Or even more sinister is the headline in the *Daily Mirror* that suggested (in November 1987) that the then Watford manager was to be replaced by David Pleat. The point was that Robert Maxwell, the *Mirror's* owner, was about to become Watford's owner (but that did not materialize)—was this paper speculation or a command from the top? Shades of political 'off the record' reporting... 'sources close to the prime minister...' Jimmy Greaves goes as far as to claim that, in the tabloids, the sub-editors write the headlines, and the poor reporter has to find the story ... we all need the gift of discernment in sports reading as well as political reading ... Furthermore, how much does the presence of the media encourage violence?

Commercial

On the other hand much of today's sport reflects commercial values, and this is true not only of what might be the so-called 'professional' sports, but even of the 'amateur' ones as well. How much are we being manipulated by the desire of someone to make money out of us? Why can we no longer go jogging without an expensive jogging-suit or digital wrist-watch? There has been the humbug of 'shamateurism' in certain parts of such so-called 'amateur' sports like Rugby Union right from the beginning (especially in South Wales). In fact, the bigger echelons of rugby are now very dependent on spectator/advertising/sponsorship cash. Who controls our sport? One report suggests that British sport now has sponsorship to the tune of £146 million a year. This presumably means less control by those inside the game and more by those outside, who want to use it for their own ends. Sport is indeed a serious affair now. We are not yet at the stage of the USA where owners of clubs can move them lock stock and barrel across thousands of miles for commercial reasons and ignore the local support that has grown up over the years—but who knows? Or consider this scenario—to change the club's strip every few years will mean the pressure on hard up parents to supply their youngsters with the latest version of the club strip. My son's Brighton and Hove Albion kit is obsolete—the sponsor on the shirt has long since gone! 'Sport for all' was the slogan of the 1970s—but certain sports require a massive investment of money and time which many can neither afford nor be given. Certain sports will always tend to be rich men's games that only highlight differences in society.

5. 'LIKE WAR WITHOUT KILLING'
Violence in Sport

Many would question the cult of violence linked to some modern sport (or is this merely a revival of violence attached to many ancient sports that went on at such places as the Colosseum?). This violence can be looked at on a variety of levels:

Firstly, has the desire to win at all costs produced violent people whose instincts need firm handling? To cite one example against many—Bobby Robson[1] relates a terrifying incident when having put the Italian club Lazio out of the EUFA cup in the Olympic stadium (7 November 1973) his Ipswich team had to barricade themselves in their dressing room against a vengeful Lazio team. It was a violence that had started on the pitch—one Ipswich player saw his career end that day. One may say that this is an example of pressure getting out of control—there is no real reason for it. Sporting officials must play their part in keeping discipline. But what message does the England team give them when it uses a player in a recent match who on the domestic level is actually suspended? One may be even more cynical, and say that some sports pander to our worst tastes by indulging in such incidents for the publicity and interest and drama's sake.

But, secondly, many would say that certain sports by their very nature are absurdly violent. Games like American football and ice hockey show, by the kind of protection the players have to wear, that violence is part of the script. It is true that the puck in hockey is hard but the fast body contact which inevitably leads to flare ups is calculated to bring on violence to the enjoyment of the public. To watch an international rugby scrum on a large video screen is quite an alarming proposition as one sees the almost casual brutality going on. Boxing, of course, has brought upon itself much opprobrium over the years with the fairly clear evidence of brain damage (and even death) from the constant blows to the head. However, one has to be self-critical here—many supporters of the sport would see opposition partly on 'class' grounds. It is mainly a working class supported sport and has often given a person from a poor background his only way up in the world.

The chicken-and-egg question about violence in sport is this—does violence in sport encourage violence on the terraces or are both reflections of society? To have lived in Liverpool at the time of the Heysel stadium disaster is an experience that I can never forget, as a pool of silence descended on the city for a while. Sadly this most grievous of disasters was one of a succession of (lesser) disasters linked to the English soccer fan.

English soccer still lives with the after-effects. In fact, violence amongst spectators is nothing new—just think of Rangers-Celtic matches over the years. Worse disasters have occurred in South America (why are so many of their stadia so designed with barriers and even water between spectator and game?) (the same week as the Heysel tragedy ten were killed in Mexico City trying to get into their cup final). Even for a Christian it is hard to make sense of this. We must try to subsume our prejudices and gut-reactions (lest our reaction is crude and violent as those whom we deplore). Are we looking at class differences, with the inarticulate expressing themselves in the only way they know?

[1] A. Barker *Time on the Grass* (London, 1982).

One set of researchers investigating 'skinheads' of Spurs matches noted that most of them came from working class estates with little future and little stake in society. The 'ends' of grounds are their territory, for which they fight on tribal grounds. But this can be too simplistic—there is evidence of quite sophisticated gangs who plan their soccer terror—people who are employed, sometimes with quite responsible jobs. And it is spreading to other sports. And again, violence in the last century's games was also quite tremendous.

The challenge to us as Christians is to be careful in drawing judgment—beware of being too individualistic and let us see violence in its societal place. We cannot just ask questions of sport as if it existed in a vacuum—it must reflect society as a whole.

Military
Looking at the part that sport plays in society also suggests to many a link with the military—a violent link indeed. One hears of games being called 'war'. American football apparently really became the American game during the Vietnam War and is clearly very aggressive/military in its play. Terminology like 'offensive' and 'defensive' have military connotations. One Max Rafferty says about opponents of the game (Gardiner *op. cit.*)... 'critics of football are krooks, crumbums and commies, hairy loud-mouthed beatniks. Football is war without killing'. Physical education has long been associated with the military, and without doubt in the Iron Curtain countries the link with the military has been very strong. Leading sporting heroes hold nominal army jobs whereas their main role is to increase the prestige of regiment, army or nation.

6. 'OPIATE FOR THE MASSES'

Christians and Sport

Our discussion may indicate why Christians have been uneasy over the question of sport, though reasons may vary from group to group.

1. For many Christians life is seen as a preparation for eternity and thus there are more important things to worry about other than sport and leisure in general. There is the whole question here of the puritan 'seriousness' of the Christian life and its outcome. This view was very understandable in ages when the mortality rate was so high that our modern notions of fitness were simply not applicable. Life is in these circumstances a vale of tears compared with the joys ahead beyond the grave.

2. Leisure/sport leads to bad habits: 'Satan finds work for idle hands'.

3. Leisure/sport leads to bad company. Dr. Crane, a USA Methodist, complained in the 1860s that players of baseball (a game then in its infancy) were recruited from the 'idle shiftless and yet ambitious class of mortals'. Clearly here is class snobbery and this surfaces also in England. The attack on cruel sports in the early nineteenth century, highlighted by the RSPCA, was seen by the working classes as an attack on their class, and not least because fox-hunting and the like were not the subject of censure.

4. Among certain Christian groups there is an unease with the 'unpredictability' or 'spontaneity' of sport and allied leisure pursuits. There are calls for moderation and no excesses, but one feels that gaiety is not to be encouraged. Unpredictability contrasts deeply with ideas of discipline that we have inherited from our forefathers.

5. Amongst more sect-like groups time for sport is simply squeezed out by the amount of religious activities. It is not that sport *per se* is rejected but that it has a low priority. (One sees this also in some modern Religious Movements such as the Unification Church). There is neither time nor energy available.

   This was also a reaction to the 'Catholic looseness' or 'latitudinarian indifference'. Christianity must stand out as being uncontaminated by the world. The world is seen in very unsubtle ways—not this or that, but a whole rejection of society around a sport, and a retreat into a 'pure church'.

6. The Sabbath question has been a stumbling block for many Christians since the reformation. It surfaced with the puritans and again in the nineteenth century and still has its influences today. The revival of evangelicalism in the late eighteenth century led to the formation of the Lord's Day Observance Society (1833) which has kept the

'OPIATE FOR THE MASSES'

pressure on society to maintain a Jewish-sabbath-type Sunday. John Loweson[1] charts the gradual retreat of the sabbatarians in the nineteenth and twentieth centuries on this score. The village in Suffolk where I was vicar a few years ago had, even after the last war, the village playing field locked on Sunday (the power was in the hands of the local chapel). The dilemma has been graphically portrayed in *Chariots of Fire* with the refusal of the hero, Eric Liddell, to run his heat on the sabbath in the 1924 Paris Olympics.

This sabbath question raises the issue of class differences. E. R. Wickham brings this out well.[2]

Sheffield men requested the opening of the free library on Sunday because that was their only free time. The Rev. Brewin Grant reacted that opening the library would be . . . 'only the first act in opening the floodgates of dissipation, irreligion and open profanity' and sarcastically denounced the men's ability and motives.

One suspects that this attitude to the sabbath goes with a bunch of other attitudes of unease with sport, recreation and leisure. It reveals a deep insecurity about society, not least its lower orders, and how it will operate.

7. The link with gambling also has made Christians uneasy down the ages, though it is probably fair to say that most Christians can enjoy sport without the resort to gambling if they so desire.

8. Sometimes the church has been concerned with the brutality of certain sports, and the physical damage that can ensue, but this of course can be grossly exaggerated. One writer complained that roller-skating led to cases of heart, kidney and other organic diseases being much exacerbated and anaemia of the most intractable sort!

One could say much more—not least about the role of women. How little I notice is expressed about women and sport in the readings concerning the puritans. Or, furthermore, the even graver misgivings by many Christian writers in the nineteenth century who may have had certain reservations about men and sport, but for women it was beyond their understanding. The myth of the gentle woman at home (which had been fed by the cult of the home by second and third generation evangelicals) led to fears of all sorts of physical and mental damage to the health of such dainty flowers and the dangers to their moral well-being. The cause of women athletes has been hindered even today by the legacy of such thinking.

So how did Christians react to the rise of modern sport and leisure? A writer comments about the nineteenth century . . . 'thus the church came to allow the legitimacy of leisure but there were still many conditions

[1] *British Journal of Sport Science.*
[2] E. R. Wickham, *Church and People in and Industrial City* (Lutterworth, 1957).

they attached to its pursuit.' What some call the sanctified recreation, quoting the Lichfield Church Chronicle of 1852 '. . . an important part of the church's mission is to leaven and sanctify the amusements of the people'[1]

Yes, amusements are allowed but they must have a rational reason— chess and reading were fine, some might allow cricket or walks, and Charles Simeon, the doyen of evangelical churchmen in the early nineteenth century, said 'exercise, constant, regular and ample is absolutely essential to a reading man's success.'

The church then tried to use sport to preach a message via 'muscular Christianity', and provided facilities such as the 'mission' in the poorer parts of towns with their links and staffing from the public school élite. This was an accommmodation which in the end could not dam the tide, partly because people did not want the church to control their leisure and partly because of lack of finances. Today the church cannot compete with the municipal sports centres.

So, in the end, there is a cultural time-lag. Christians accept that sport/ leisure is as much part of reality as work, marriage, or any other facet of life. The Christian duty is now to be leaven in the lump or to be salt and light, by individual and corporate activity and reflection upon their involvement. An organization such as 'Christians in Sport' seeks to bring together Christians in professional sport as a pastoral support of like-minded people and to help them use their careers for the gospel. The era of Christian imperialism is over.

Has Sport Replaced Religion?
These last remarks lead naturally to the question of how much has mass-attended sport (and to some extent sport in general) replaced much of the traditional values and emotion and signs of religion. Have the deep-seated affections of the masses been won for a secular enterprise?

Robert W. Coles highlights in a tentative (and tongue in cheek?) way the parallels between religion and sport.[2] He notes the set ritual before the games, the almost liturgical chants, the mass mutual identification between players and supporters, the use of religious type words like 'worship'. With the bigger clubs this can be a deep-seated feeling that this is the focus of life. One Liverpool fan (who was doing some building work on our house) confessed to getting really tense (stomach upsets) within a couple of days of a big game. Coles draws parallels with revivalist meetings.

A Christian will be suspicious of 'idolatry', though he will also recognize the overuse of religious metaphor. He may also confess the distance between organized religion and popular culture and the reasons that have caused it. He may see this 'worship' as something trivial, which asks no deep questions of life, but simply is a big escape if it is taken to its full conclusion. He may also ask about certain religious activities in the past— were they merely providing the kind of escape which now has been secularized.

[1] Eileen and Stephen Yeo, *Popular Culture and Class Conflict, 1590-1914* (Harvester Press, Sussex, 1981) p.115.
[2] R. W. Coles 'Football as a Surrogate Religion' in Michael Hill (ed.) *A Sociological Yearbook of Religion in Britain* No. 8 (SCM, 1975).

'OPIATE FOR THE MASSES'

Another 'secularized' religious achievement of sport is said to be 'reconciliation'. People point to troops playing football between the trenches on Christmas Day 1914. Religion was the spur, but sport the means of this short reconciliation.

One could say that certainly the troops wanted to express their mutual misery but on the whole this all seems very superficial. My wife remembers the disgust of a Suffolk policeman sent to Toxteth after the 1981 riots, when he and his colleagues played football with the black people of Toxteth and were roundly abused by their Liverpool colleagues.

Or there is the case where differences can lead to differing sporting codes e.g. the origins of Rugby Union and League over broken-time payments to northern factory players. The more middle class 'union' members for whom this was not an issue (being wealthy) broke the unity of the game. Underlying was sheer snobbery—complaints about the northern 'warped sporting instinct.' Arthur Budd, president of the RFU in 1888, claimed that sport was a matter of 'disinterestedness' yet complained that the northern paid players were the best: which showed that he was concerned about who gets the glory. This snobbish attitude remains to the present day. Any Union player who turns 'professional' with the League becomes a social outcast.

Can we erect a theology of Sport?
Sport as we know it is largely a nineteenth century phenomenon. One looks in vain for a blueprint in the Bible about sport (as about so many issues). What we can do is look at the biblical picture of reality and see how our modern life fits in.

For instance, there is a high view of the physical body in the scripture which for many centuries has been obscured by a Greek body-soul dualism. The body is seen as a unity—Genesis 2.7, man *becomes* a 'soul' (Heb: *nephesh*) rather than *has* a 'soul'. He is a unity of matter (from the earth) and spirit and the matter part is not despised as inferior to some 'spiritual' side. The fact that our Lord is seen as healing bodies should also underline this. In the largely agricultural society of biblical times, the body was exercised literally in work. A wholesome body is admired. One can think of the young man Saul (1 Sam 9.1-2). Sexuality is a wholesome expression of the person (Song of Solomon). So the body is good and wholesome.

One can perhaps see the rise of sport in the light of working and societal changes in the nineteenth century. Long hours at work in factory or office do not give the body the dignity it deserves.

Sport fills a gap that the new society has created. And as Christians have come to terms with sport and sex, it is partly because they have rediscovered the biblical concept of the whole person.

Can one see our sporting events as a secular version of biblical festivals? Biblical feasts obviously had what we would call a 'religious' side to them, but also a 'secular' with their feastings and fun. These were times to celebrate, to drop out of the normal cycle of life. We hear (albeit in a slightly sordid context) of the women of Shiloh dancing at a feast (Judges 21.15-22). The 'work ethic' has to come to terms with these biblical situations of 'fun' and 'spontaneity'. And what exactly was going on at that wedding feast which our Lord's presence 'adorned and beautified' (John 2)?

We have rightly taken in the biblical view of the disciplines of life; the need to subdue the earth; the need to work (he who will not work should not eat), generally the 'serious' side of life—but are there hints of a 'less serious' side? We may not go as far as G. Stradling who describes 'fun' (*op. cit.*) as

> 'rough and ready balance in universe between chaos and cosmos—fun points up this knife edge of balance and in doing so it brings an intensity to life' (p.142).

We must also take the Biblical warnings. Sin is still in business and will corrupt anything, whether sport, politics or church life. The Lord admires the body he has made (and saw fit to be incarnate in one) but can say also that 'he has no delight in men's legs' i.e. bodily strength as a source of power in its own right that forgets the Maker.

We must remind ourselves that there is a danger of the cult of the physique—and that there is more to man than that. We must remember how the Servant—his form disfigured—lost all the likeness of a man (Isaiah 53.2 NEB)—and that true greatness in God's eyes is often so different from the world's estimate. There again, feasting and fun can be twisted and alienated from its true purpose as the prophets of the Old Testament insisted.

Paul, in the New Testament, is happy enough to use athletic metaphors even though for him as a Jew, athletics may not always have had the best connotations. The background of the Maccabean struggle for Jewish independence c.150 B.C. is the attempt by Hellenistic society to suppress Jewish religion and culture. One symbol of this Greek culture was its athletics often with accompanying nudity. The metaphor of athletics occurs in 1 Corinthians 9.25-5, Philippians 3.12-14, 2 Timothy 4.8 (if Pauline). The remarks in 1 Timothy 4.8 seems slightly to disparage fitness as opposed to preparation for the Great Day but by 6.12 Timothy is encouraged to run the great race of faith. The athletics metaphor is happily used again. Clearly for Paul, the sporting world provided useful analogues for the Christian life; and as such is not despised but does have its place and limitations. The rewards of the Christian race cannot be compared to the running race. Its achievement is soon forgotten, the prize soon withers, but what the gospel offers is something enduring.

An aspect of sport is the team or group identity. People identify with their local or national team and get excitement and a sense of pride and achievement in the team's achievement. Paul was proud of being from Tarsus 'no mean city'. Again one rests on a narrow ledge—one can soon topple over on to the dark side of all this; and chauvinism, tribalism and crude nationalism can distort what may be a healthy feeling. But that is the fate of any earthly institution or place—it may be a sign of God's providence but it can also be a sign of the demonic. One has only to compare Rome in Romans with the Rome of Revelation.

'OPIATE FOR THE MASSES'

Further; the Bible is not simply about people as individuals, it is about people in groups whether family, clan, tribe, nation, church or whatever. God made man a social being and being involved in a sport can be a reflection of this capacity of man. For a Christian the social group par excellence will be in the church but, as he takes his part in other groupings, there is no reason why he should not be part of a sporting group.

In fact a sporting group may be an expression of other relationships whether local, job or business. My job in a London insurance head office, playing for the firm team fostered a sense of comradeship and I suspect a sense of job satisfaction. For the Christian there will be the careful thinking of where his various loyalties lie and for men in general the question of family loyalties as well and the whole question of 'manhood' (see discussion under 'women').

A Christian view would want to emphasize that God is involved in all the world—for God there are no 'no go' areas. Society is structured differently from Bible times and, unless one withdraws into a 'sect' type of 'ghetto Christianity', there is going to be the painful job of working out attitudes and roles. And it is not simply a matter of reading off certain biblical insights. We have to recognize that the church cannot speak with an innocent past on these issues. It continues to live with its past failings and mistakes. Those failures are part of the national consciousness. Take for example the church's failure of prophecy in World War 1—so many clergy, chaplains and lay folk indulged in simplisitic patriotism fuelled by an equation of English sporting values, religious values and patriotism. The church always has to live with ambiguity—between what is and what should be. Our discussions have pointed out certain misgivings about sport as it has developed in our modern life—how do Christians who are involved, or who get enjoyment from watching, live with these ambiguities? It is the old question of being 'in the world and not of it'. To be a Christian is no more guarantee that a person will do well and succeed than it is a defence against illness. Presumably a Christian wants to succeed, but should he, for instance, pray for victory? A Christian may and ought to thank God for his success (Deuteronomy 8.17-18), but not that God should show favouritism to his followers.

So what is the particular contribution a Christian makes? Is it being a good sport, a good loser, and a generous winner? For the spectator, is it appreciating his own team and yet not being overcome by a chauvinism that cannot recognize the abilities of others? This may all be true, but the Christian must watch against a kind of 'priggishness'. Why should not a Christian express disappointment? Christians are a bundle of emotions like any one else and a lot of effort and hope has gone into the event.

There is the narrow tightrope to be walked between this reasonable expression and some of the 'over the top' attitudes we have discussed before. It has for instance been pointed out that Jimmy Hill, when leader of the players union, advocated stealing yards at throw-ins, but now wants

SPORT—THE OPIATE OF THE PEOPLE?

a penalty for a 'professional' foul! Do Christians 'time waste' if they are winning with only a short time to go—is this an acceptable part of the game or are we thinking still it is 'ungentlemanly'?

What about evangelism? That appears to be the goal of a recent organization like 'Christians in Sport' based in Oxford. They describe their goals thus:
> As the working week shortens and leisure time increases, sport will play a more and more important part in our lives. Christians in Sport is committed to bringing the Good News of Jesus Christ into the world of sport. We are working for the day when there will be an effective and lasting witness for Christ as sportsmen and women living godly Christ-centred lives will make a great impact on our nation and the world.'

The brochure notes that many American professional sports teams have chaplains (and there are attempts to have chaplains to English soccer clubs and no doubt in other sporting activities) and that Bible study forms an important part of any sportspeople's lives. A report of a tour to India (1985) sees the game itself as secondary and the 'witness' of the team more important:
> 'for three weeks we lived and played, and witnessed together as members of the Body of Christ, no one got drunk, no one tried to get off with a girl, no one swore, no one moaned ... what a contrast to a normal sports team.' (Newsletter No. 4 1985).

Drunkenness and wenching are not unique to sport, but it is good that a group of Christians can show that there are other values in life. Wherever we are, we are called to show that we have values based on our Lord Jesus Christ. So one trusts that Christians involved in such organizations will think through some of the wider issues connected with sport. There is the danger of being selective in what horrifies you. Ian Botham was suspended from cricket for his toying with drugs, yet members of the MCC committee have been found guilty of offences from drink driving to admitted adultery. Moreover, Botham has refused money to go to South Africa. Is not this all very selective? It is clearly right that 'Christians in Sport' (like Christians anywhere) should want to be evangelists, but there should be the aspect of Christian prophecy whereby we look for 'God at work in sport' as a part of sports expression of God's creative will. We need an 'industrial chaplaincy' approach to sport, as well as using sport for evangelism.

Are the best teams Christian teams or should Christians be individuals in secular teams? This is like the question ... do you work for a Christian firm, attend a church school, belong to a Christian political party or do you avoid these 'holy concentrations'—be 'salt' and 'light' in God's world? The sportsperson needs to think out his relationship with the world and its ambiguities—the world is God's creation and continues to be the object of his love and providence and yet at the same time 'lies under the power of the evil one'.

'OPIATE FOR THE MASSES'

For the Christian there are certain 'hot' issues such as the 'Sunday question' (raised in the *Church Times,* 27 November 1987). In this issue Simon Jones puts the case against Sunday sport. He points out the proposal to remove present restrictions on Sunday sport (e.g. to make it legal to charge admittance—at the moment legal dodges are in use) will have a big impact on the nation's life. He rightly points out that modern sport is commercial, and really the same kind of objections to commercial sport (what does he think of 'amateur sport'?) are as applicable to Christian opposition to Sunday shop opening. He notes the impact on those forced to be employed, and on family life of these and those (he assumes mainly male) who will watch. Is this a 'secular sabbatarian' defence, for the idea that Sunday is a special religious day will not have much impact on a largely secular nation? How much can the church demand of a secular nation that it should do as the church suggests?

Whatever way the church makes up its mind (and probably minds) on this particular issue, it must realize that 'one off issues' like the Sunday question cannot be treated in isolation. That's where nineteenth century sabbatarianism went wrong. It was a largely middle-class movement, oblivious (or even contemptuous) of the needs of the exploited industrialist proletariat (see earlier discussion).

The church witness in the last century was to provide sporting and leisure facilities—though often with a very definite social thinking behind it. By and large the church cannot compete with modern commercial sport and offers very inferior goods. But there may still be ways that the church can learn to 'serve' the community (or basic community) rather than 'dominate' it, especially in areas which are not able to benefit from the commercial usage. Some church buildings in our inner cities have taken on a new role by being 'community centres' and becoming relevant to local needs by providing (often in the only suitable buildings around) facilities for leisure and sport. The conversion of St. Johns Fairfield in inner Liverpool is one of many examples.[1]

---

[1] Ian Gilbert, *The Making of Post Christian Britain* (Longmans, 1980) is a good discussion of this thesis.

7. RUN THE STRAIGHT RACE-IN CONCLUSION

Sport occupies an increasingly important place in national and internatonal life (even if for many it means little). Christians are called to witness to God's creativity, love and redemption wherever they are, and that will include the world of sport. That witness will not only be evangelistic, but will also be a prophetic assessment of the values enshrined in sport, many of which derive from the cultural setting of the sportspeople. Just as in industry or politics this world has its shortcomings. The Christian must live with the ambiguity of life—a life which is both an expression of God's creativity and also human perversity since the Fall; a life hallowed by Christ's incarnation which looks forward to culmination in his second Advent.

Between these times the challenge for a Christian in sport, whether as professional, amateur or spectator, is to sanctify it and bring the mind of Christ to it. He will compete, but will respect his opponents as made in God's image; he will not let the label 'sport' blind him to the moral implications of his play; he will not overvalue the 'superstar' or mere human prowess; he will not let the rules of the game override the universal Christian rule of love, nor be happy to see people exploited by commercial or other interests under cover of sport.